God's Amazing Creations

by

James Christian

Empyrion Publishing
Winter Garden, FL

ISBN: 978-0692296707

Empyrion Publishing
PO Box 784327
Winter Garden, FL
Info@EmpyrionPublishing.com

Unless otherwise noted, all Scripture quotations are from the King James Version of the Bible.

Printed in the United States of America

PREFACE

These selected poems tell of my walk of faith as a Christian. I spent the first 42 years of my life with the name "Christian," living in sin and for myself. I am glad to say that for the last 25+ years I have enjoyed a new nature, being born-again into the kingdom of God.

Love is a verb to me, so I have compiled and arranged these verses to tell the wondrous story of God's grace and love which brought me personally to salvation and faith in Jesus Christ.

This *faith* has brought such joy into my life and caused me to learn and apply new wisdom to it. This *faith* has much *hope* instilled within it's message and has taught me to set goals and to pursue them.

And now in me abides *faith*, *hope*, and *love*. Of the three, the greatest of these is *love*.

As you read these verses, may your mind be renewed with the overwhelming love of your Creator. Where I could, I have given the scripture references that inspired that particular piece of poetry.

Every Christian has a testimony. This is mine. This book is dedicated to the God of my salvation. May it be a true blessing to you.

James Christian

TABLE OF CONTENTS
God's Grace

Salvation

New Understandings

Reaching Forth

What Remains

God's Grace

THE GOSPEL
Revelation 22:17

The gospel invites all to come;
Come, come to God's kingdom.
Come to the Father through Jesus the Son:
The work is finished, all is done.

This is grace, what the faithful believe;
It's not what they do, but what they receive.
Where God in them makes a change
For those who believe in Jesus' name.

For God has dealt with death and sin,
So that all men may come to Him
By giving them new life in His Son,
To those who believe that the work is done.

Nothing for them to do but live and grow
In Christ, from whom all blessing flow.
To love, and by loving God know.
To live. To die. To God's kingdom go.

GOD'S AMAZING CREATIONS

Beginning Creation–Heaven and Earth

From His heart, the Word
Was breathed and given birth,
And God was heard
Creating Heaven, creating Earth.
God said, and it was.
The Word formed His thoughts,
God is the Eternal Cause
That made something out of naught.

Creation of Man–Adam

The Word not used in forming man:
Adam made by God's own hands,
But the Word was put within
With breath of life given him.
Man is made a living soul
From things natural and spiritual.
In God's image, full of glory,
First Adam starts the human story.

Creation of Woman/Bride

In darkness deep, did Adam sleep.
He needed help–God saw the need.
Man shouldn't be alone, so God took a bone
From Adam's side, and created for Adam a bride.
Pronounced them as one flesh–Man and Wife
And sent them forth to multiply,
To keep and dress a garden,
A paradise called Eden.

Sin Altered God's Creations

Sin is the lack of faith and love,
To obey and follow God above.
Introduced by Satan's pride and deceit
Who would have all bow at his feet.
Sin kills the senses of man, steals his fruit,
Destroys fellowship with God, man, and Truth.
The Adams sinned, God's image destroyed;
But God promised a new creation to employ.

New Creation–Heaven with Earth

From His heart, the Word
Was breathed into a womb
And conceived, awaiting birth.
God and the seed of woman,
Heaven's Glory in cursed Earth,
A new creation was begun:
Emmanuel, Jesus, God's salvation,
God's only begotten Son.

The Creator's Life

Given life, He showed us heaven,
Taught it's Truth, showed us God.
Flesh, Satan's world for sin,
Under His foot was trod.
No, Satan had nothing in Him.
He had a life, free of sin.
The Lamb of God could be sacrificed
And on a cross was crucified.

The Creator's Death–Our Atonement

At the cross, Satan was judged.
We must see sin and self as dead.
At the cross, God shows us His love,
By putting sin on His Son's fleshly head.
We must see Christ crucified to live again;
For at the cross, new life begins.
We must God's work believe and confess,
For God to put His Spirit in us.

Creation–Second Adam

Second Adam began in death
Where perfected by His obedience,
God raised Him up to eternal life:
Sin's perfect sacrifice.
Glorified, the clay removed,
Replaced by the celestial.
Love tested, tried and proved:
Second Adam is made spiritual.

New Creation–Church/Bride

From darkness, out of His side
From water, blood, death and sin
Came forth second Adam's Bride.
Cleansed and spiritually born-again,
Enabled to keep and dress her garden.
Rejoicing, she explains her pardon,
Telling all of God's Kingdom,
Inviting all to come.

New Creation–Heaven and Earth (Future)

The last creation will be the best,
The redeemed enter into God's rest,
Into a new Heaven, a new Earth,
Glorified in their new birth.
Made one with Him, in the New Jerusalem,
They live and reign with Him
And they shall see God's face,
The final act of God's grace.

ONENESS

One God who made Adam and Eve.
One disobedience. One act of sin
From one law. From one tree,
Separated the oneness of God and man.

God created both good and evil;
And over both only He has control.
Eve was deceived by Satan, the Devil;
Adam ate willfully, damning the soul.

Good replaced Godliness, a self-righteousness;
Man lost truth, gone was His faith.
Evil brought death through its corruptness;
Man sought his own love and grace.

Gone was the glory of God's creation,
The image of a Holy God, gone!
Naked without God's glory came confusion,
So that fig aprons were sewn and worn.

One disobedience. One act of sin.
From one law. From one tree,
Came separation, the oneness of God and man.
One Holy God, who made Adam and Eve.

There are laws that teach right from wrong,
Laws that separate the evil from the good,
Laws of forgiveness for what man has done,
Laws based on the atoning blood.

To Adam, God gave the law of atonement;
But the law can never give life.
It only lasts for a brief moment,
Brings peace, rest from strife.

So God also gave hope, restoring man's faith.
The hope of One, who was to come:
Whose life swallows up death
And restores to God the kingdom.

But man did not manage good or evil,
His flesh was too easily drawn away.
He failed trying to resist the Devil.
He lived not for tomorrow, but for today.

Man tried through the ages, in all generations
To be like his Maker, while his Maker he denied.
Few lived in faith, made God their salvation,
Trusted fully in Him, gave God their lives.

One baby born in a manger to a virgin,
Born to Joseph and Mary, who beheld the promised Seed
Of a Son of God, and a Son of Man,
From the promise given to Adam and Eve.

One baby in the form of sinful flesh
That hid the Word…The God within.
One baby that grew, and who would bless
God His Father and all men.

This baby is Jesus, the Messiah,
Who received from God His Holy Spirit,
To perform His ministry for Jehovah
When baptized in Jordan's River.

Reunited, the Spirit and Word with man became one,
Performing signs and wonders that were to prove
Jesus was the Messiah, God's only Son.
This led to a cross to prove His love.

One Cross. One death. One Resurrection.
Things that fulfilled all of God's law,
That completed God's plan for salvation,
That can restore all that's been flawed.

God kept His promise, the promise has come:
And with it better promises in life.
For God gave us His only begotten Son,
And to believers, the Spirit of Christ.

God's plan of eternal salvation
Is that we, with Him, be made one.
And to complete our restoration,
Is Christ Jesus. God's will. God's Son.

Our salvation, God put in our hearts to follow,
To be worked out until we all go home
To His kingdom, which is so hallowed
In victory, for His will is done

Through one God and Father of all:
One Lord. One Spirit. One Faith.
One Hope in which we are called.
One Baptism. One Body. One Grace.

NOTE:

There is only one remedy for the effect of the Tree of Knowledge of Good and Evil on mankind...

...the other tree in the midst of the Garden – the Tree of Life – the Cross, on which the Lord Jesus Christ was crucified.

PUT A MIRROR ON A CROSS AND...

*L*ook, look, look at the face
Then remember Jesus took your place.
God took all our sins
And put them all on Him.
Get this in your heart and head:
Jesus died, but He's not dead.

With Christ are you crucified?
Into His death been baptized?
See the mirror, see your face,
See His body bearing your disgrace.
Death for sins you have done,
Your shame borne by God's Son.

Look, look at salvation's cost.
Find new life at His cross.
Believe that He died for you.
It starts here for me and you:
Don't hold on to self and sins,
Stop here – give them to Him.

Look, look, look and remember why,
Listen to the Lord Most High.
Receive this message from above,
Full of God's amazing love:
Confess, what God has already done,
Receive new life in His Son.

It doesn't matter how good you've been,
God has concluded all have sinned.
This is the grace of God and His Christ:
Your sin is forgiven, Jesus paid the price.
Take Him as Savior, make Him your Lord.
Listen to God, obey his word.

Arise, arise and be baptized
To eternal life in Jesus Christ.
Receive His Spirit and follow Him,
Be alive to God – dead to sin.
Give God thanks for this grace:
That Jesus Christ took your place.

Salvation

MY REPENTANCE

I was lost, when I heard His voice
Calling me, and I made the choice
To answer Him, and I said, "Yes Lord."
But from Him came no other word
So I carried on in my usual ways,
Thinking that my mind had played
Some kind of trick on me…
What could the Lord want from me?

He called again, in sweeter tones
Another day, while I was alone
Planning my tomorrows, but without Him.
My life was filled with lust and sin:
In fact, my flesh had complete control,
And smothered the cry of my soul.
"Not now Lord," I sighed,
And once more was God denied!

I lived in sin for quite a while…
Playing in it like a child,
Never giving it a second thought
That one day, I might get caught.
And that day eventually came…
And I had to face the shame
Of going to prison for my sins.
Hey, where is God? I've need of Him.

Where are you God? I've need of you.
Isn't there something that you can do?
I'll go to church and say my prayers
If you will get me out of here!
But God, He refused my deal
And I lost my first appeal.
Yet God, He called again to me…
What does the Lord want from me?

So in prison, I did sit and pout…
Because God wouldn't get me out.
While my soul cried from deep within…
"Help yourself and search for Him."
How? Where? I didn't know the way…
Where to go… or what to say.
I tell you, I was in misery
Trying to solve this mystery.

Now the Bible is one of those books
Into which I had never looked.
But somehow I sensed a need…
So I found one, and began to read
About the Lord, and I found out
Just what God was all about...
And why the Lord would call to me
And why he never answered me.

I found that God, He hated sin,
But wanted me to worship Him.
So bad had He desired my love
That He had sent His Son, down from above
And there, at a place called Calvary…
He died, and shed his blood for me:
To free me from the power of sin,
To cleanse and make me whole again.

How guilty and worthless I felt
As on the prison floor I knelt.
And with tears, I repented for being wrong
As I prayed to God, whom I had shunned.
"Forgive me God," that was my plea.
"Come and cleanse and sanctify me."
I want to change my way of living...
Please forgive all of my sinning.

Well, Alleluia! Praise the Lord!
God heard me…every word.
Jesus came and changed my being.
He has changed my way of living.
Christ, who is my righteousness
Teaches me His holiness.
I am learning every day…
How to live the Christian way.

I've been blessed and I've found peace...
And from my prisons, I'm now released.
I now serve my risen Lord,
Abiding daily in His word.
And I know the reason why
God waited for my right reply.
Yes, God who created Earth and Heaven,
He hates sin, but loves the sinner!

NEW BIRTH

I've had my little Bethlehem,
Coming forth a new creation,
For I have received of Him
Through death, a resurrection.
And day by day, in sweet communion,
I grow into his perfection.
For I'm the Lords, and He is mine,
And this is Love's desire…
That with His glory, I may shine
In His glorious attire…
And this will be, when all of me
Is pruned and purged with fire.

MY CONVERSION

On the night of my conversion there was a great spiritual battle that decided the destiny of my soul. These visions of the Rope, of Hell, of the Cross, Happiness, and The Revelation of Jesus Christ, happened that night:

Vision 1: Satan wanted me dead! He showed me a rope. I had been contemplating suicide. I was disgusted with my life. My pride wanted the pity of others. Besides, I had found no relief in the Bible I was reading... only sin and a God who hated it.

Vision 2: God showed me Hell! A fearful sight. I changed my mind about suicide. I became afraid of death, and of God.

Vision 3: Satan then offered me a life filled with riches, power, and sex. "You might as well live it up," he said, "while you are still alive."

Vision 4: God showed me a cross. I knew it was mine. Fear and dread swept over me. Then I saw someone else hanging on that cross.

Vision 5: God gave me a revelation of Jesus Christ. I saw Him hanging on that cross, dying for me. Paying the sin debt to God with His life, His blood. My sight became faith, and I believed.

A miracle happened – I died and I was "born-again." God won. I was saved. Get behind me Satan – I now follow Christ.

SOMEONE WANTS ME DEAD

Inspired by My Conversion

Someone wants me dead!
I don't want to die.
I'm not crazy in the head.
Neither do I lie.
Someone wants me dead.

Someone wants me dead.
Death torments my mind.
Death is something not to dread
For death would be kind.
Someone wants me dead.

Someone wants me dead.
I see my escape plan:
A cross, God's plan for the dead,
Salvation for the damned.
Someone wants me dead.

I am not afraid!
I have found a substitute:
Jesus, the one who saves
And gives life, it's truth.
I am not afraid.

I am not afraid.
I will not be scared.
I have seen Hell's fiery grave,
Bodies burning there.
I am not afraid.

I am not afraid,
My soul will live on.
My life ends not at the grave.
My soul to God belongs.
I am not afraid.

THE CALL TO FREEDOM

I had no hope when in prison,
My life was full of self and sin.
In myself was all the wrongs
Of every evil I had done!
And in my torment there I cried
"I am no good! I want to die!"

Praise God, He has a better way:
(I still died, but live today).
He showed me that all was not loss,
And my identity in a cross,
Where His Son died for sin and me
To give me life, His life, eternally.

Self, my only prison that bound my soul,
Christ freed, and prison gates unrolled.

THE ONLY GOOD SINNER

The only good sinner is a dead one!
Where rigor-mortis does it's job,
Mortifying the deeds of the fleshly one,
Who has been born again by God.
Spirit filled, he is a saint
Pleasing both His God and man,
One that has no complaints.
A sinner freed from sin,
A saint is truly a holy one
Restored to God through Grace.
Seated with Christ on His throne,
Envisioning that heavenly place
He abides, living among mortal man
Loving, 'till Christ comes again.

JOY

Luke 15:25

There's music in my Father's house.
The servants dance and sing,
The walls with alleluias ring.
His Son has changed his point of view,
His servants rejoice now at the news.
There's music in my Fathers house.

There's music in my Father's house
For each son that does return.
The love of God forever burns
To all who change their point of view
And make response to His gospel news.
There's music in my Father's house.

There's music in my Father's house.
As in heaven, so in earth,
We praise God for all we're worth.
We sing, we dance, we shout,
That's what rejoicing is all about.
There's music in my Fathers house.

New Understandings

THE LORD'S SUPPER
I Corinthians 11:23-26

The Lord Jesus the same night in which he was betrayed took bread: and when He had given thanks, He brake it, and said, Take, eat: this is my body, which is broken for you: this do in remembrance of me. (I Cor. 11:23-24)

Bread broken did not mean his bones,
Broken meant separation blood from flesh:
Blood for our sins to atone
Payment for sin, to save us from death.
The blood, His blood, was for the Father alone,
His blood saves from God's holy wrath.

After the same manner also He took the cup when He had supped, saying, This cup is the New Testament in My blood: this do ye, as oft as ye drink it, in remembrance of me. (I Cor. 11:25)

The blood separated from the God/man
As it flowed from His pierced side:
The blood for God, the water/spirit for men.
This is the new covenant for which He died,
The blood for the remission of sin,
The Spirit of Christ to make the dead alive.

For as often as ye eat this bread, and drink this cup, you do shew the Lord's death till He come. (I Cor. 11:26)

Jesus came not to make bad men good
But to make the dead alive.
He gave His body and His blood
For us to have new life.
This message must be understood:
That death, by His death, brings life.

MY NAME IS...
Philippians 2:13

I come from God, yet never leave Him
I'm described as breath and wind
And sometimes I'm called fire
Because I bring and stir God's desire.
I am the carrier for the Lord
'Cause I bring forth His word
I've been known as Inspiration
But I'm really into transportation
For I move man and mountains.
I do the flow of God's fountain
And if you drink of His river of truth
I will bring forth the fruit.
I bring life and destruction
I also do resurrections
I can do all things but sin
For I'm a holy part of Him.
I come from the Father, through the Son
All because of what Christ has done.
Sometimes I am known by His name
Because He bore your sin and shame
I bring spiritual gifts from them
For you and for all men
So that God's work can be done
Follow me, as did God's Son.

Join your will unto mine
I'll bring you to God divine.
Resist Me and I can
Return you back to Satan.
Now if there be any glory or praise
Any thanksgivings or anthems raised
Let them go back to My source
To God, my eternal power and force.
He dwells in you, lives in Heaven
And I by Him am given.
"Will, will of God" is my name
I'm the one who brings a change.
But I'm misunderstood the most:
Because I'm called the 'Holy Ghost.'"

YE HAVE HEARD

John 4:34

*Y*ou have heard, "You are what you eat."
To do the Father's will was Jesus' meat.
He discloses something we did not know,
That doing God's will sustains our growth.
Jesus proved He was God's Son
For in God's Spirit, God's will was done.
Our maturity into the stature of Christ
Is done by living a Spirit filled life.
The Lord's Supper, our communion
Reminds us, we are not alone.
Bread and wine, though His death it shows,
Enables us to do His will and grow.
So in Christ to be complete
Remember, "You are what you eat."

HE SPEAKS

John 16:4,16

*H*e is the Good Shepherd who knows His sheep
And to each of us He does speak;
Into our hearts His love He instills
Enabling us to do The Shepherd's will.

We are the sheep of His flock
And on His words we take stock;
So no matter where we go
Our Shepherd's will we will know.

PRAYER LIFE

*P*rayer warriors arise equip'd to win
Their course for the day is prepared:
To go to sinners, who still sin,
To preach a word, received in prayer,
To love, and present Jesus to them.

They have a shared life in their prayers
As the burdens for others they feel.
Through God they seek another's care
As before God's throne they kneel,
And His will for others they find there.

God does not hide or withhold
From them that pray His will
And love as they've been told.
His presence abideth with them still
As His plans for others, He unfolds.

Boldness comes, all fear is gone,
God's love in their hearts is instilled.
There are no wants in God's kingdom.
Each day His children are filled,
Each day God's will is renewed and done.

MY WALK

Sometimes I gaze towards the sky
And ask the Lord the reason why?
Of things that I don't comprehend,
To help me learn and understand.
Sometimes I stop in unbelief
And go to Him for my relief
To ask if this is the right way.
Or have I somehow gone astray?
My life 'tis given to His care
So I commune with Him in prayer.
My faith is in Him, and not in me
To solve my life's perplexities
I trust in Him to see me through
The way I go, and what I do.

MY WALK II

Some men know less, some men know more
But all are brothers, that's for sure.
Encourage each, uplifting them:
Know them in Christ, not as men.
Walk in obedience to what you know,
God gives increase… you will grow.

VOICES

Oh the noise of many voices
Calling, pleading, for our choices.
"Come" they say, and some say "Go."
Temptations toss us to and fro.
But in the midst of this storm
Is a voice cool and calm,
Instilling peace into our hearts
If from Him, we do not part.

Such is the voyage of this trip
For those who ride faith's ship.
Waves of discouragement, fear and pride
Can only beat upon its sides.
Sealed this boat is with His blood
And held securely by His love.
Yes, we are on a stormy sea,
On our voyage to eternity.

FORGIVING

Self-pity is a weed in the garden
Of a heart that does not pardon,
A bitter weed that has anger as it's root:
That grows revenge as a shoot,
Which blossoms fruits of malcontent,
Wrath, and hatred, and resentment.
Only your prayer of forgiveness
Removes the weed of bitterness.
Draw on the strength of Jesus' name.
Remove the weed, make the change.
The only pity a Christian needs
Came from God in His mercy.
So be bold: In Christ be strong,
Endure with patience others' wrongs.

FORGIVENESS

Forgiving is for giving – Give!
Jesus forgave, then gave His life
And by His death, gave us life.
Give Life – Go forgive – Live!

Love covers many a sin – Love!
God so loved, and gave His son;
Jesus died, God's will was done.
Give life – Remember the blood – Love!

Sinned? Need forgiveness? Ask!
You can't receive your forgiveness
Until sin, your wrong, is confessed.
Get life – confess, repent – Ask!

Chains binding your heart and soul? Forgive!
Bound on earth, bound in Heaven;
Loosed on earth, loosed in Heaven.
Forgiveness – frees your soul – Forgive!

PRAISE THE LORD

Alleluias are forever; amen and amen.
That's why we sing them, again and again.
"Praise the Lord" is what it means!
Praise to our God and King.
Alleluias are forever; amen and amen.

Endless grace, endless love that proves
Endless life, endless wisdom from above.
An eternal God who makes all things new
For us to have, to live, and to do.
Sing forth His praise – allelu, allelu!

This is worship as God we praise,
The highest glory man can sing,
As our thankfulness we raise
To God and Christ the King.

GOD'S HOLY TEMPLE
Revelation 21

Holy is God who made us,
Holy, He who loves us so.
Holy is His Son Jesus
Of whom each saint is made whole.
Grace is that we are forgiven
Made holy ones without blame,
Bound by love for His heaven
In Christ Jesus' precious name.
One body with Christ as head,
His church awaits to go home.
A live church amongst the dead,
A church made of living stones.
This is God's New Jerusalem:
It is us! God's forever home.

Reaching Forth

PLANTING GUIDE
I Corinthians 3:11-15

God has made this our lot:
Each of us plants a crop.
By our crops we are known,
Crops don't come 'less they're sown.
And we reap what we sow:
From good seed, good things grow;
From the bad, fruits of sin.
Our harvest tells what's within.
Plant good seed in your field
And good fruit you will yield.
Then when the fields are gleaned,
Brought before our Lord and King,
He won't find in your share
Thorns and thistles, weeds or tares,
And you'll receive His reward
For sowing seed from His word.

NAVIGATION

Navigators will take the time to stop
And take their current bearings;
Or else they might end up lost
From the error of their steering.

They set a course towards a spot
And head out in that direction;
But, no matter how carefully they plot,
Their course will need correction.

For no one goes from "A" to "B"
And keeps a line that's straight;
For courses are altered when at sea
By the tide, and winds, and fate.

Like good navigators we must be,
Our ways in life we should check:
To be where we want to be…
Ourselves, we should introspect.

Our courses they may be true,
So might be our intentions,
But we should watch what we do
If we are to reach our destination.

For heaven's road is very straight
And the road is very long.
God's spirit will take us to the gate,
Correct and convict where we've gone wrong.

But man can fall short of their destination,
Even fall from God's love and grace;
Because they don't correct their navigation,
They end up in the wrong place.

It does not mean they're not saved,
But have missed the first resurrection.
Their bodies sleep within their graves
Waiting for the final resurrection.

So steer according to His truth,
Checking your course in prayer.
Seek His directions when lost or confused,
Follow His way 'til you get there.

THE RACE TO PERFECTION
Phil. 2:12-16

I have the vision of that heavenly place,
A place called the New Jerusalem
And I have entered perfection's race,
And shall run in it 'til it ends.
God has given me the power to win it
By covering my sins with His blood.
He's filled me with His Holy Spirit
So I run in faith, hope, and love.

Paul said, "Run that you may attain."
That means some attain not.
Some are held back by the world or by gain,
Some look back, like the wife of old Lot.
But to the city of refuge I am fleeing,
From the world and the curse of the law
And into God's Kingdom I am pressing
'Til my last breath, I have drawn.

RACING REVIEW

*A*nother week has come and gone,
And I have done much better than some,
Yet failed in respect to quite a few
But each new day I start anew.
It's been a week of fiery trials;
Some I passed, and some I failed.
Seems always so in this heavenly race:
You win a crown, but are saved by grace.
The object of this race is to finish,
Complete the course, and diminish
The works of flesh and finish first.
Being conformed into our Christ,
That's whose life our lives are meant to be,
Completely changing our personalities
Into His, whose life was given
That we might live with Him in heaven.
Christ has risen from the tomb.
I fear not failure, nor doom,
Though I may fall a thousand times
He will help me to the finish line.
This week, I'll consider it as training,
That I might finish the course remaining.
My course in life, I shall complete
And when it's finished, bow at His feet,
In praise and loving gratitude
For all that He has led me through.
To Him, I'll give my victor's crowns,
I cannot claim them as my own,
For it will be His love and grace
That helped me finish my heavenly race.

Some running tips, I'll give to you,
For you have entered this race too.
Begin each day upon your knees,
Always believing in His victory.
On your knees, you cannot stumble
On Satan's tricks that makes one tumble.
Lift your eyes to the finishing line,
Trust in Jesus, you'll do fine.
Keep the Bible as your guide,
Avoid all paths that are wide.
Keep to the narrow and the straight,
Until you reach the pearly gates.
God shall supply all your needs
To run your life abundantly.
So, keep your tank full of oil,
Don't run out, or you'll be foiled
And left outside of the wedding.
That is the prize we are pursuing.
This racing review now ends:
Remember, you're running with friends.
Run in His power, which is love,
'Til you reach your goal above.

God Speed.

ANOTHER YEAR

Another year of waiting,
In hope, anticipating;
Staying in the Word,
Waiting for our Lord.
Prayers are always given
For saints, and the sinner,
Yet my heart does yearn,
For the Lord's return.
Keeping on in fellowship,
In duties and in worship;
Waiting 'til He comes,
Comes to take us home.

PREACHING THE CROSS

Many are the issues of today
And man is with opinions swayed.
Sides are taken, lines are drawn.
What is right? And what is wrong?
But problems, they still remain
Because man, he does not change.
For in man lies all the wrong
For every evil ever done.

Hopeless? No! All's not lost
There's the preaching of the "Cross."
There the Lamb for sinners slain
Bore man's sin and rose again.
There by God, can sinful man,
In mercy, be "born-again."
Solve the issue, end the strife
Enter rest, and find true life.

RIVER OF LIFE
John 7:38; Revelation 22:1

Want to do something for God's Son?
Open your floodgates, let the river run.
Don't be like the old Dead Sea,
Keeping all that it receives.
Let the river run it's course
Always remembering it's source.
If something is blocking the flow
You are to blame, to the cross go.
Guard well your relationship to Jesus Christ
And there will be a steady flow for other lives.
God's Spirit is not to be stored.
Be like the Lord, be out poured.
Issue the invitation for all to come.
Complete your mission let the river run.

What Remains

SILENT WITNESS
GOD'S LOVE

"I love you." Three little words
Never uttered by our Lord,
But shown to us from creation,
From life to death, and in redemption,
For actions speak louder than words.
Look at the works of the Lord,
How He meets all our needs.
Love is the action. Love His creed.
His love is seen, but never heard,
Recorded for us in His word
As an example on how to live
In Love! A love that gives.
The expression, "I love you,"
Is not to say, but to do.

A VOCAL WITNESS
MY LOVE

The day of your salvation has come.
Will you confess–Jesus is God's Son
And believe what has been done?
Then live your new life as one
In Christ, for God's kingdom.

If so, turn the page and see the cross,
And you in Jesus, who paid the cost.
The last verse has your instructions
To grace, to glory, to God's salvation.

PUT A MIRROR ON A CROSS AND...
MY IDENTITY IN HIM

*L*ook, look, look at the face
Then remember Jesus took your place.
God took all your sins
And put them all on Him.
Get this in your heart and head:
Jesus died but He's not dead.

With Christ you are crucified
And into His death been baptized.
See the mirror, see your face,
See His body bearing your disgrace.
Death for sins you have done,
Your shame borne by God's Son.

Look, look at salvation's cost.
Find new life at His cross.
Believe that He lives for you.
He rose again to bring this truth.
Thank Him for being born-again
And for paying for your sins.

Look, look and remember why.
Listen to the Lord Most High.
Receive this message from above,
Full of God's amazing love.
Confess what God has already done.
Live the new life in His Son.

It doesn't matter how good you've been,
God has concluded that all have sinned.
This is the grace of God and His Christ:
Your sin is forgiven, Jesus paid the price.
Take Him as Savior, make Him your Lord.
Listen to God and obey his word.

Arise, arise and be immersed
In eternal life in Jesus Christ.
Obey His Spirit as you follow Him.
Be alive to God – dead to sin,
And give God thanks for this grace:
That Jesus Christ took your place.

KNOW

John 1:14; John 5:39-40

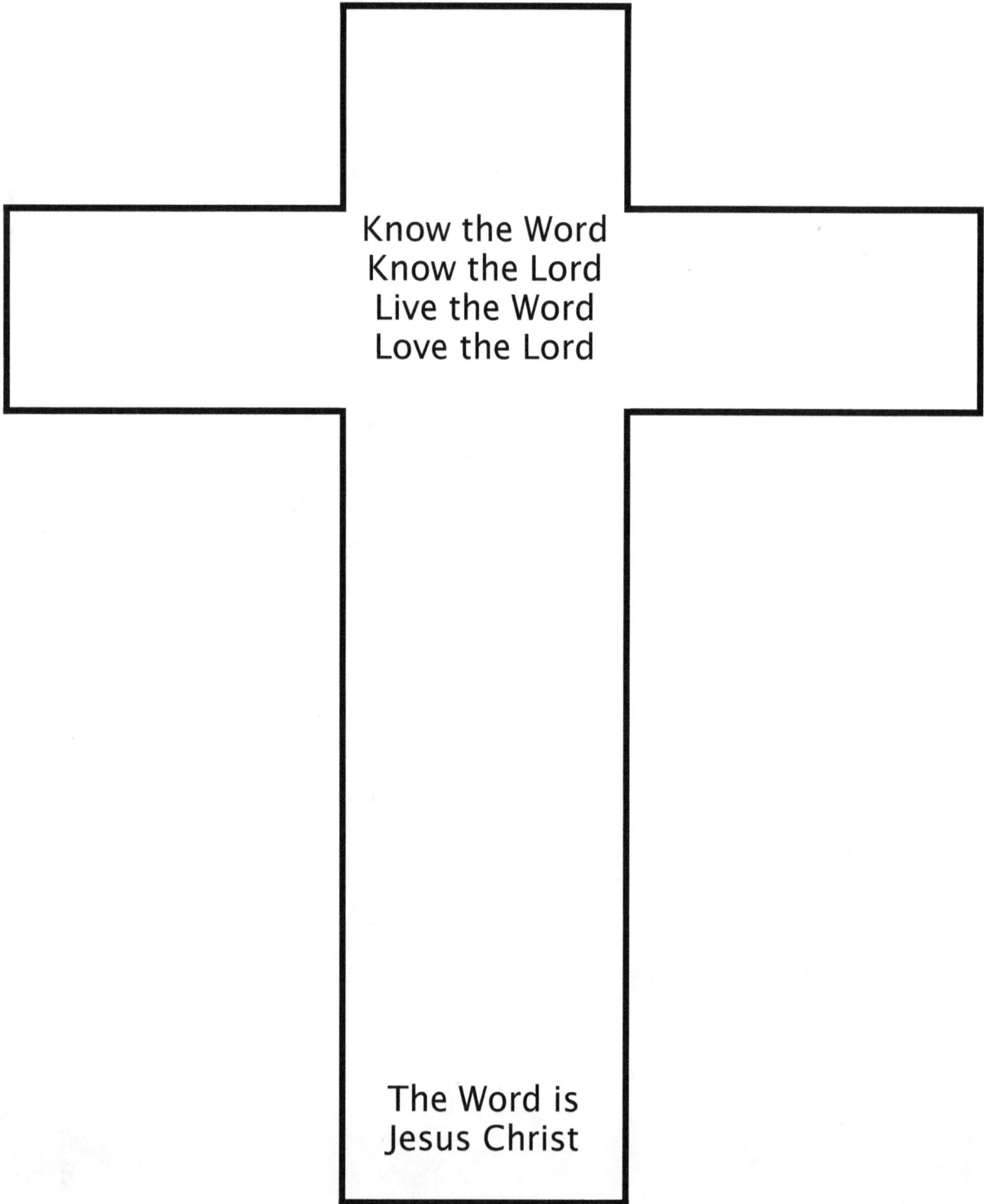

Know the Word
Know the Lord
Live the Word
Love the Lord

The Word is
Jesus Christ

I LIVE
MY LIFE IN HIM

I live in the glory of my Lord
In light veiled by the flesh.
His life and mine are in one accord.
My life shows forth His death
To things not of His kingdom,
Until the day He comes.

I live in the glory of my Lord,
To the highest I can attain.
'Tis a life in accordance to His word,
A life He and I maintain
To glorify our Heavenly Father
Who bids me come, rise up higher.

I live in the glory of my Lord:
Christ Jesus is His Name.

www.ingramcontent.com/pod-product-compliance
Lightning Source LLC
Chambersburg PA
CBHW081539040426
42447CB00014B/3437